Sports Illustrated KIDS

THE EVOLUTION OF

BASKETBALL

by Matt Doeden

CAPSTONE PRESS
a capstone imprint

Capstone Captivate is published by Capstone Press, an imprint of Capstone.
1710 Roe Crest Drive
North Mankato, Minnesota 56003
www.capstonepub.com
SPORTS ILLUSTRATED KIDS is a trademark of ABG-SI LLC. Used with permission.

Library of Congress Cataloging-in-Publication Data is available on the Library of Congress website.
Names: Doeden, Matt, author.Title: The evolution of basketball / by Matt Doeden.
Description: North Mankato, Minnesota : Capstone Captivate is published by Capstone Press, [2022] | Series: Sports Illustrated Kids: Ball | Includes webography. | Includes bibliographical references and index. | Audience: Ages 8-11 years | Audience: Grades 4-6 | Summary: "How has the game of basketball changed since it was first invented? In more ways than anyone back in 1891 could have ever imagined! Discover how a simple game played with peach baskets evolved over time into the complex sport we know and love today"-- Provided by publisher.
Identifiers: LCCN 2021015986 (print) | LCCN 2021015987 (ebook) | ISBN 9781663906557 (Hardcover) | ISBN 9781663920676 (Paperback) | ISBN 9781663906526 (PDF) | ISBN 9781663906540 (Kindle Edition) Subjects: LCSH: Basketball--History--Juvenile literature. | National Basketball Association--History. | Women's National Basketball Association--History.Classification: LCC GV885.1 .D632 2022 (print) | LCC GV885.1 (ebook) |DDC 796.323--dc23LC record available at https://lccn.loc.gov/2021015986 LC ebook record available at https://lccn.loc.gov/2021015987

Image Credits
Alamy: FL Historical 1A, (bottom left) Cover, FL Historical 1A, top 1, 6, Hum Images, 7; Associated Press, 15, Alvin Chung, 22, John Locher, (middle right)Cover; Getty Images: Bettmann, 8, 11; Library of Congress: Johnston, Frances Benjamin, 9; Newscom: Everett Collection, 12, KRT, 17, Manny Millan/SI/Icon SMI, 25, Sotheby's/Goldin Auctions/MEGA, 21, Stephen M. Dowell/ MCT, 13; Shutterstock: Africa Studio, (writing) design element, Chamnong Inthasaro, (court) design element, ChromaCo, (silhouette) Cover, Dan Thornberg, (ball texture) Cover, EFKS, (arena) design element, Rawpixel.com, 27, Stephen Marques, (court lines) Cover, SvgOcean, (basketball word) Cover, teka12, (girl) Cover; Sports Illustrated: Bob Rosato, (middle left) Cover, David E. Klutho, 29, John G. Zimmerman, 16, John W. McDonough, 5, Manny Millan, 18, 20, 24, Robert Beck, 26, Walter Iooss Jr., 19

All internet sites appearing in back matter were available and accurate when this book was sent to press.

Printed and bound in the United States of America. PO4270

TABLE OF CONTENTS

Words in **bold** are in the glossary.

THE FANS GO WILD

Steph Curry spots up. He drills a long three-pointer. Swish! Sue Bird takes a bounce pass as she comes off a pick-and-roll. Zion Williamson soars through the air. He throws down a slam dunk.

These are the kinds of plays that bring basketball fans to their feet. The modern game is filled with fast-paced action. Yet for much of the sport's history, none of these plays even existed. There were no alley-oops. The game did not have **crossover** dribbles. There were no match-up zone defenses. It has taken nearly 130 years for the game to grow into what fans love today.

Golden State Warriors guard Steph Curry (#30) rises up to take a shot in a game against the San Antonio Spurs.

CHAPTER 1

FROM PEACH BASKETS TO THE MODERN GAME

Fans would barely recognize the sport when it was first played in 1891. Each team had nine players. They hurled a soccer ball at peach baskets. The baskets were nailed onto walls. Every time someone made a basket, they would have to climb up to get the ball out of the basket. The first games featured men. But women started playing the game less than a year later.

Dr. James Naismith invented the game of basketball in 1891. The early game featured peach baskets.

Naismith (middle row, right) poses with his first basketball team.

The early game was slow. Teams did not score many points. It probably was not much fun to watch. It is amazing that the game grew to become the popular sport that it is today.

Basketball first appeared in the Olympic Games in 1936. The U.S. men's team is pictured here.

Big Changes

The new game quickly grew popular. But it took time for it to look like the game that fans watch now. Backboards first appeared in 1895. Dribbling the ball became legal in 1901. At first, the rules allowed players only one dribble before they had to pass or shoot. That one dribble had to bounce over the player's head!

In 1936, men's basketball was at the Olympic Games for the first time. By this time, the game and rule book had **evolved** into something close to the modern sport. And yet, the game's evolution was just beginning.

COLLEGE BALL

The first known college basketball game was played in 1895. Teams from Hamline University and the Minnesota School of Agriculture in Saint Paul, Minnesota, faced off in the basement of Hamline's science building. The visiting team won, 9–3.

The first women's game came a year later. Stanford beat the University of California by the whopping score of 2–1!

Jump-Starting the Game

Basketball in the 1920s was slow-paced. The game was a low-scoring grind. Players shot the ball from a flat-footed stance. The shots were easy to defend. Offenses struggled to score.

But all of that changed in 1936. Stanford player Hank Luisetti worked on a new type of shot. It would change the game forever. Luisetti's running one-handed shot was instant offense. It transformed the game almost overnight. The game's action was faster. The scores were higher. A new era of basketball had begun.

Hank Luisetti's (#7) shot evolved into the jump shot, a staple of the modern game.

CHAPTER 2

CHANGING TIMES, CHANGING GAME

College ball was the peak of the sport for many decades. That started to change in the 1940s. The National Basketball League was formed in 1937. The Basketball Association of America was formed in 1946. In 1949, the two pro leagues joined to create the National Basketball Association (NBA).

Center George Mikan was the NBA's first true superstar.

Stars drove the league from the very start. The first NBA superstar was George Mikan. He played for the Minneapolis Lakers. Mikan was big and strong. He dominated the game. The young league had to invent rules just to slow him down. For instance, the goaltending rule was made because of Mikan.

Goaltending, illegal in the NBA, is when a defensive player touches the ball while it is above the cylinder of the rim.

GOALTENDING

A rule barring defensive goaltending changed modern basketball. However, goaltending is legal in Olympic competition. The rule says that a defender cannot touch a shot that is on its way down toward the hoop. But the rule wasn't always part of the game. For more than 50 years, defenders were free to pluck away shots at any time. The new rule helped boost scoring—and excitement—in the game.

A New Wave

Basketball was changing. But so was society. Racism was a big problem in the United States. People of color were fighting for rights they had long been denied. Things slowly changed. That was true in basketball too.

In 1950, Earl Lloyd became the first Black player in the NBA. Lloyd broke the NBA's color barrier. He paved the way for future stars who would transform the league. Those players would spend decades fighting for equal treatment on and off the court. But the league was no longer limited to only white players.

Earl Lloyd (#11) was the NBA's first Black player. He helped pave the way for a new generation of basketball stars.

The Slam Dunk

The **jump shot** changed basketball in the 1930s. A new kind of shot made its mark in the late 1950s and early 1960s. It was the slam dunk.

Players had dunked as early as the 1940s. But the dunk became a force of the game when stars like Bill Russell and Wilt Chamberlain entered the league in the late 1950s. Their dunks rattled the rims. Dunks electrified crowds like no other shot. The game was played above the rim for the first time.

Center Wilt Chamberlain reaches for a rebound.

Bill Russell (left) and Wilt Chamberlain (right) battle near the basket.

Magic Johnson (#32) lofts a shot in a game against the Philadelphia 76ers.

CHAPTER 3

MAGIC, BIRD, AND A NEW GAME

In the 1970s, the NBA was struggling. Fans were drawn to college basketball, as well as other sports. The TV ratings were falling for NBA games. The league needed to be saved.

Earvin "Magic" Johnson and Larry Bird were the men to do that. Johnson and Bird had been **rivals** in college. They entered the NBA in the late 1970s. They brought a new swagger to the league. Their rivalry made the NBA more popular in the 1980s. Fans could not wait to see Bird's Boston Celtics play Johnson's Los Angeles Lakers. The TV ratings of these games soared. And a new era of the NBA was born.

The Houston Rockets' defense presses in on Boston Celtics star Larry Bird (#33).

Air Jordan

Bird and Johnson may have saved the league. But another player took it to a new level. Michael Jordan had it all. He could drive the ball. He could step back and shoot from outside. He was **elite** on the defensive end too. Jordan was a big-time winner. He led the Bulls to six NBA titles in the 1990s. Fans loved him.

He had his own line of Nike shoes. He appeared in ads for everything from soda to underwear. Jordan's face was everywhere. The NBA's popularity grew and grew. For many fans, Jordan remains the greatest player ever to play the game.

Michael Jordan (#23) drives into the lane.

IT'S GOTTA BE THE SHOES!

No piece of sports fashion has made a bigger splash than Nike's Air Jordans. They were first released in 1985 with a price tag of $65. The shoe quickly became an iconic part of popular culture. Fans lined up to buy each year's new release. Even long after Jordan's retirement, Air Jordans remained one of the biggest pieces of basketball style in the world. In 2021, the sneakers sold for $170 for the basic sneakers up to $2,000 for specialty versions.

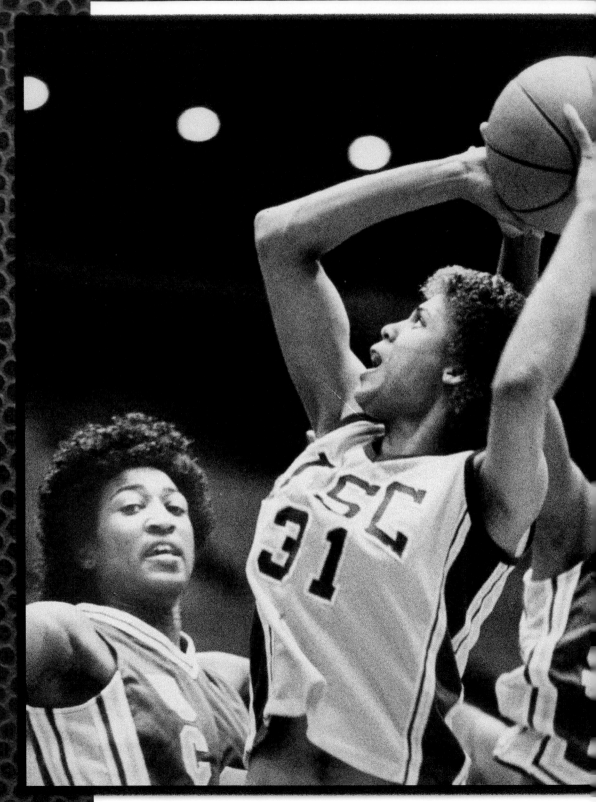

She Got Game

The men's game grabbed most of the headlines. But quietly, the women's game grew more popular too. A wave of female stars took over the college game. They did the same on **international** teams too. Cheryl Miller and Sheryl Swoopes thrilled fans. Fans loved to watch their slick ball-handling and dead-eye sharp shooting.

Several pro leagues for women came and went. But women were laying the groundwork. They were building a fan base. And something big was about to happen.

USC's Cheryl Miller (#31) was an unstoppable force in college in the 1980s.

CHAPTER 4

THE MODERN GAME AND THE RISE OF THE WNBA

Women's basketball was a huge hit at the 1996 Olympic Games. U.S. fans were excited as they watched Team USA win the gold medal. Their success caused NBA owners to form a new league. They created the Women's National Basketball Association (WNBA).

The U.S. women's team won gold at the 1996 Olympics, helping to ignite interest in women's basketball.

The league began to play in 1997. Cynthia Cooper played for the Houston Comets. She and the team dominated the league early on. The WNBA game featured crisp passing and accurate shooting. The women showed strong **fundamental** play. Over the next three decades, the league grew. Stars such as Candace Parker, Maya Moore, and Sue Bird thrilled fans. They showed that the women's game was here to stay.

The age of the three-pointer

By the 2010s, the NBA was taking on a similar look. Powerful players such as LeBron James still ruled the court. But a new style was taking over. Pure shooters such as Steph Curry launched three-pointers at a record pace.

Steph Curry waits to show off his skills at the All-Star Weekend Skills Challenge.

Meanwhile, many NBA teams looked to **analytics**—the study of deep, detailed statistics—to drive the style of play. And the analytics were clear. Three-pointers and dunks were the most **efficient** shots in the game. The mid-range jump shot had been a big part of the game for decades. But a new way of playing had taken over. The mid-range shot was becoming a thing of the past. Teams around the league sought out the world's best long-range shooters.

NEW AGE STATS

For almost a century, basketball stats were about points, rebounds, and assists. But in the modern NBA, analytics has produced new, advanced ways to measure performance. New-age stats such as the Player Efficiency Rating (PER) and win shares (a stat that measures how much a player contributes to winning games) rate players on almost every move they make—from defensive ability to how they move without the ball. These new stats allowed coaches to find strengths and weaknesses that traditional stats didn't reveal.

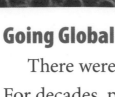

Going Global

There were other changes too. For decades, players born in the U.S. dominated the NBA. But more international players were changing the face of the league. These players included Germany's Dirk Nowitzki, Greece's Giannis Antetokounmpo, and Australia's Lauren Jackson. The international players took the U.S. by storm.

The new wave of talent made the NBA and WNBA truly international leagues. They helped shift the focus of the game to a style built around the three-pointer. They have played a big role in the ever-changing style of basketball in the U.S. and beyond. Fans can only wonder what the game will look like in 20, 30, or 50 years!

Dirk Nowitzki (left, center) helped make the NBA a truly international sport.

GLOSSARY

analytics (AN-uh-lit-iks)—the study of deep, detailed statistics, which is used to form strategies

crossover (KROS-oh-ver)—a dribble in which a player quickly changes direction by quickly dribbling the ball across his or her body

efficient (ih-FISH-uhnt)—productive and not wasteful

elite (ih-LEET)—describes players who are among the best in the league

evolve (ih-VAHLV)—change over time

fundamental (fuhn-duh-MEN-tuhl)—a basic skill of a game, such as dribbling and shooting

international (in-tur-NASH-uh-nuhl)—including more than one nation

jump shot (JUMP SHOT)—a basketball shot taken mid-jump

rival (RYE-vuhl)—team or player with whom one has an especially intense competition

READ MORE

Doeden, Matt. *The Great Ones.* North Mankato, MN: Capstone, 2022.

Jankowski, Matthew. *The Greatest Basketball Players of All Time.* New York: Gareth Stevens Publishing, 2020.

Schell, Matt. *NBA and WNBA Finals.* Minneapolis: Lerner Publications, 2021.

INTERNET SITES

NBA
nba.com/

SIKids Basketball
sikids.com/basketball

WNBA
wnba.com/

INDEX